Fantastic Gree
with Po

Ellen Mollenvanger

FORTE PUBLISHERS

Contents

ISBN 90 5877 637 9

This is a publication from
Forte Publishers BV
P.O. Box 1394
3500 BJ Utrecht
The Netherlands

For more information about the creative books available from Forte Publishers:
www.forteuitgevers.nl

Final editing: Gina Kors-Lambers, Steenwijk, the Netherlands
Photography and digital image editing: Fotografie Gerhard Witteveen, Apeldoorn, the Netherlands
Cover and inner design: BADE creatieve communicatie, Baarn, the Netherlands
Translation: Michael Ford, TextCase, Hilversum, the Netherlands

Preface

Do you also like to look at all the different types of contour sticker? I come up with new ideas of what to do with them every time I look at them. And then, unexpectedly, I was asked to write a book about contour stickers. So, here it is, my first book, Fantastic Greeting Cards with Peel-offs.

Once you start, you will not be able to stop, because new ideas will keep coming to you. As you can see, there are countless possibilities using all the different types of attractive paper.

I hope that you have as much fun as I did using contour stickers.

Have fun!

Ellen

Many thanks to the Reinders family for having faith in me and José Smits for her offer to help and her critical opinion.

Techniques

Sticking large stickers on the card

It is often difficult to stick large stickers on paper so that they are nice and flat. To do this successfully, carry out the following. Draw the shape of the card on a piece of paper. Next, mark the place, as a mirror image, where you want the sticker. Place the sticker with the sticky side facing upwards on the place you have just drawn. Carefully lower the card (within the lines drawn on the paper) so that the sticker is loosely stuck on the card. Turn the card over and carefully press the sticker into place.

Choosing a colour of mother-of-pearl paper

The different colours of mother-of-pearl paper are different to distinguish between, because their colour changes depending on the lighting. In order to see the true colour, hold the sheet of paper against your waist. You will then be able to see the colour by looking downwards along the paper.

Sticking stickers on mother-of-pearl paper, illusion paper and circle paper

These types of paper have a structure to which photo glue does not stick very well. Therefore, cut double-sided adhesive transparent foil into strips or use double-sided adhesive tape. If you wish to tear these types of paper, then remember that the circle paper is difficult to tear.

Materials

- Papicolor paper and card
- JEJE fantasy paper
- JEJE illusion paper
- JEJE circle paper
- JEJE mother-of-pearl paper
- JEJE contour stickers
- JEJE text stickers
- JEJE cutting sheets
- JEJE double-sided adhesive transparent foil
- Paper cutter
- 3D tweezer scissors
- Sandy-Art knife

- Cutting mat
- Ruler
- Photo glue
- Silicon glue and a syringe
- Foam tape (1 mm, 2 mm and 5 mm)
- Chalks
- Organza ribbon
- Eyelets
- Gold thread
- Satin ribbon (7 mm)
- Double-sided adhesive tape
- Glaze Gelly Roll pens

- Tweezers
- Eraser
- Pencil

Papicolor has card and paper of the same colour. It is often handy to use card to make the card itself and paper for the pieces which are stuck on the card, because then the card will not be so heavy.

All the article numbers are given with the instructions for the cards.

Step-by-step

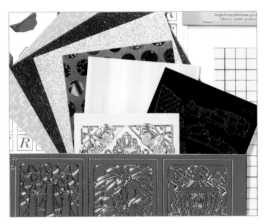

1. Paper and sticker sheets.

2. Place the sticker upside down and then stick it in place.

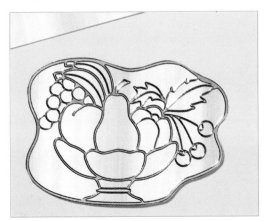

3. Stick the stickers on different types of paper and cut them out.

4. Put all the pieces together on the card together.

Cards on pages 1 and 3

Card on page 1

What you need
- Papicolor card: ice blue (42)
- JEJE illusion paper: 85740
- JEJE fantasy paper: 85510
- JEJE sticker: multicolour/white boats 12472

Instructions
1. Cut, score and fold an ice blue double card (14 x 14 cm).

2. Cut a square (13 x 13 cm) out of illusion paper and a square (12 x 12 cm) out of fantasy paper. Stick the squares on top of each other and then stick them on the card.

3. Cut four squares (5 x 5 cm) out of illusion paper and cut four ice blue squares (4.5 x 4.5 cm) and stick them on top of each other.

4. Stick a picture of a boat on three squares and stick the text on the other square. Stick two squares flat on the card and use foam tape to stick the other two squares on the card.

Card on page 3

What you need
- Papicolor card and paper: dark blue (06)
- Papicolor paper: ice blue (42)
- JEJE mother-of-pearl paper: 85140
- JEJE circle paper: 85340 and 85300
- JEJE 3D sticker sheet: gold 21100

Instructions
1. Cut, score and fold a dark blue double card (13 x 13 cm).

2. Cut a square (12 x 12 cm) from mother-of-pearl paper, an ice blue square (11 x 11 cm) and a dark blue square (10 x 10 cm). Stick all the squares on the card.

3. Stick the largest 3D sticker on blue circle paper and cut it out in a circle. Stick it on ice blue paper and cut it out leaving a 2 mm border.

4. Stick the second 3D sticker on gold circle paper, the third 3D sticker on blue circle paper, the fourth 3D sticker on gold circle paper and the last 3D sticker on blue circle paper. Cut them all out and use them to make a 3D star. Stick the circle in the middle of the card and stick stars in the corners.

Animals

Dolphins

What you need
- Papicolor card: ice blue (42)
- JEJE mother-of-pearl paper: 85060
- JEJE cutting sheet: 33360
- JEJE sticker sheet: dolphins 13430
- JEJE text sticker

Instructions

1. Cut, score and fold an ice blue double card (10.5 x 14.8 cm).

2. Cut the dolphins and the background out of the cutting sheet. Make the picture 3D and stick it in the bottom right-hand corner.

3. Stick three dolphins on mother-of-pearl paper. Cut them out and use foam tape to stick them on the card. Stick some small stickers and a text sticker on the card.

Animal fun

Instructions

1. Cut, score and fold a double card (10.5 x 21 cm).

2. Cut three openings in the front of the card 1.5 cm from the bottom (4 x 4 cm on the left and right-hand sides and 11 x 7 cm in the middle).

3. Cut a piece of mother-of-pearl paper (21 x 10.4 cm) and stick it behind the front of the card. Cut two cornflower blue squares (3.5 x 3.5 cm) and a corn- flower blue rectangle (6 x 10 cm) and stick them in the openings.

4. Stick two penguins, two sharks, some air bubbles and a text sticker on the card.

What you need

- *Papicolor card:*
  cornflower blue (05) and ice blue (42)
- *JEJE mother-of-pearl paper: 85000*
- *JEJE sticker: dolphins/sea animals 11372*
- *JEJE text sticker*

Noah's Ark

What you need

- *Papicolor card:*
  night blue (41) and pieces
  of pale yellow, lilac and
  sea green
- *JEJE fantasy paper: 85510*
- *JEJE mother-of-pearl paper:*
  85040
- *JEJE sticker sheet:*
  Noah's Ark 14110
- *Eyelets: dark blue*

Instructions

1. Cut, score and fold a night blue double card (13 x 13 cm).

2. Cut a square (12.3 x 12.3 cm) from fantasy paper and use eyelets to attach it to the card.

3. Stick the rainbow on mother-of-pearl paper, the ark on night blue paper, the giraffes on pale yellow paper, the elephants on sea green paper and the doves on lilac paper and cut them all out.

4. Use pieces of foam tape of different thicknesses to stick everything on the card. Stick the animals on the card so they slightly overlap each other and add a text sticker of your choice.

Flowers and butterflies

Yellow butterfly

What you need

- Papicolor card:
  lemon (09) and snow-white (30)
- JEJE mother-of-pearl paper: 85070
- JEJE illusion paper: 85700
- JEJE sticker sheet: butterflies 12550
- JEJE text sticker
- JEJE sticker sheet:
  flowers and dots 14170

Instructions

1. Cut, score and fold a double lemon card
   (10.5 x 14.8 cm).

2. Cut a square (7 x 7 cm) out of mother-of-
   pearl paper and a snow-white square
   (6.5 x 6.5 cm). Use foam tape to stick them
   on the card standing on a corner.

3. Stick a butterfly on illusion paper and cut
   it out. Bend the wings and use foam tape
   to sticker the butterfly on the square.

4. Use flowers and dots to decorate the card.
   Stick two text stickers on the card.

Pastel flowers

Instructions

1. Cut a lilac rectangle (25 x 13 cm) and score and fold it 12 cm from the edge so that the back is 1 cm longer than the front.

2. Stick flower stickers on fantasy paper. Stick a contrasting colour in the centre of the flowers and cut them out. Use pieces of foam tape of different thicknesses to stick the flowers on the card so that they overlap each other.

3. Stick the text sticker on the inside of the card on the piece that protrudes and add some small flower stickers.

What you need

- *Papicolor card: lilac (14)*
- *JEJE fantasy paper: 85500*
- *JEJE sticker sheet:*
  large cream, salmon and lilac flowers 14810
- *JEJE text sticker*

Flower with a butterfly

What you need
- *Papicolor card: salmon pink (25)*
- *JEJE illusion paper: 85710*
- *JEJE cutting sheet: 34024*
- *JEJE lace border sticker: violet 725*
- *JEJE butterfly sticker: 12550*
- *JEJE text sticker of your choice*

Instructions

1. Cut, score and fold a salmon pink double card (14.8 x 21 cm). Score the front of the card 5.2 cm from the side, 3.9 cm from the top and 3.9 cm from the bottom so that 7 cm remains in the middle.

2. Cut 3.5 cm along the top score line towards the middle fold and do the same for the bottom score line. Cut the 7 cm between the ends and fold the front of the card forwards along the score line. The rectangle will now protrude.

3. Cut out a bouquet of flowers, make it 3D and stick it on the rectangle. Stick the butterfly sticker on illusion paper and cut it out. Bend the wings and use foam tape to stick it on the front of the card.

4. Stick a lace border sticker inside the card and, if you wish, cut out the openings. Add a text sticker.

Butterflies with lace

What you need

- Papicolor card:
  lilac (37) and cream (27)
- JEJE mother-of-pearl paper:
  85020
- JEJE sticker sheet:
  butterflies 12550
- JEJE lace border sticker:
  cream and lilac 14700
- JEJE text sticker of your choice
- Glaze Gelly Roll pen

Instructions

1. Cut, score and fold a lilac double card (13 x 13 cm). Cut a square (13 x 13 cm) out of cream card and stick it in the card.

2. Stick a yellow lace border sticker on both sides of the card and cut out the openings.

3. Stick a lilac lace border sticker on both sides of a cream rectangle (13 x 7 cm). Cut along the wavy edge and, if you wish, cut out the openings. Use foam tape to stick the rectangle on the card.

4. Stick two butterflies on mother-of-pearl paper. Cut them out and use foam tape to stick them on the cream rectangle. Use a glaze pen to draw a dotted line behind the butterflies and stick a text sticker in the middle.

Marriage

Bride and groom

What you need
- JEJE transparent sheet
- JEJE mother-of-pearl paper: 85000
- JEJE sticker sheet:
  bride and groom 13701
- JEJE sticker sheet: bells 13371
- Glaze Gelly Roll pen:
  various colours

Instructions

1. Use a transparent sheet to cut, score and fold a double card (14.8 x 10.5 cm). Cut a piece of mother-of-pearl paper (14.8 x 10.4 cm) and stick it inside the card.

2. Stick two wedding bells on the mother-of-pearl paper.

3. Stick the bride and groom and a flower border on the front of the transparent card.

4. Use glaze pens of different colours to colour in the stickers.

Swans

Instructions

1. Cut, score and fold a lilac double card (13 x 13 cm).

2. Cut a square (12.5 x 12.5 cm) out of illusion paper and a square (12.5 x 12.5 cm) out of circle paper. Cut them into two triangles and stick the triangles irregularly on the card so that all the sections are of a different size. Leave a space of 2 mm between the sections to stick a holographic line sticker.

3. Cut a lilac square (8.5 x 8.5 cm) and cut a triangle (8 x 8 x 11.4 cm) out of illusion paper. Stick the triangle on the square and use foam tape to stick them on the card.

4. Stick a swan sticker on the square. Stick another swan sticker on a transparent sheet and cut it out. Use silicon glue to stick the transparent swans slightly in front of the other swans.

What you need

- *Papicolor card: lilac (14)*
- *JEJE illusion paper: 85710*
- *JEJE circle paper: 85350*
- *JEJE transparent sheet*
- *JEJE sticker sheet: multicoloured swans 13120*

Invitation

What you need
- Papicolor card: pale yellow (29)
- JEJE mother-of-pearl paper: 85000 and 85060
- JEJE transparent sheet: 31000
- JEJE sticker sheets: bride and groom 13701 and window 14621

Instructions

1. Cut, score and fold a pale yellow double card (13 x 13 cm).

2. Place the window sticker on the card upside down (with the sticky side facing upwards) and use a pencil to draw the outline. Cut out the outline of the window and cut the same shape out of a pale yellow square (13 x 13 cm).

3. Cut a square (13 x 13 cm) out of a transparent sheet and stick the transparent square behind the front of the card. Stick the sticker in the opening on the transparent square. Cut the two windows open and fold them outwards. Stick the pale yellow square inside the card to hide the transparent square.

4. Take a sticker of a bride and groom and cut the bride and the groom from each other. Stick them on mother-of-pearl paper and cut them out. Stick the groom on the card and use foam tape to stick the bride on the card. Position them so that they can both be seen through the window.

Silver wedding anniversary

Instructions

1. Cut, score and fold a salmon pink double card (14.8 x 10.5 cm). Score the front of the card 5.3 cm from the fold and fold the front outwards.

2. Cut two strips of blossom card (3 x 14.8 cm and 5 x 14.8 cm) and two strips of mother-of-pearl paper (4 x 14.8 cm and 6 x 14.8 cm) and stick one on top of the other. Stick the wide strip of mother-of-pearl paper on the inside of the card and the narrow strip on the front of the card.

3. Stick the wedding cake on mother-of-pearl paper. Cut it out and stick it in the middle of the wide strip. Stick the "25" sticker on a blossom circle (Ø 5 cm). Stick it on a mother-of-pearl circle which is 2 mm bigger and then stick it on the card.

4. Use sticker shapes to decorate the card and stick a text sticker inside the card.

What you need
- Papicolor card:
  salmon pink (25) and blossom (34)
- JEJE mother-of-pearl paper: 85010
- JEJE sticker: wedding patterns 11111
- JEJE sticker: anniversary numbers 10961

Birth

Dummies

What you need
- *Papicolor card:*
  lemon (09)
- *JEJE illusion paper: 85700*
- *JEJE sticker sheet:*
  dummy on a stamp 12010
- *JEJE lace border sticker:*
  cream 14670

Instructions
1. Cut, score and fold a lemon double card (13 x 13 cm).

2. Use lace border stickers to divide the card into four and cut out the openings in the lace.

3. Stick four dummies onto illusion paper and cut them out.

4. Use foam tape to stick them in the four sections.

Baby washing

What you need
- Papicolor card: lilac (14)
- JEJE fantasy paper: 85500
- JEJE sticker sheet: multicoloured baby clothing 14002
- JEJE text sticker: pink 11502

Instructions

1. Cut, score and fold a lilac double card (14.8 x 10.5 cm). Stick a piece of fantasy paper (14 x 10 cm) and a lilac rectangle (5 x 10 cm) on the card.

2. Stick the washing line on the card and hang the washing from it.

3. Stick two clothes hangers with a piece of washing line above the rectangle.

4. Stick small stickers in the corners of the card and a text sticker below the rectangle.

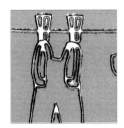
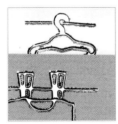

Baby bear

What you need
- *Papicolor card: light blue (19)*
- *JEJE scrapbook sticker:*
  blue bear/heart 19254
- *JEJE sticker sheet:*
  various borders 13230
- *JEJE text sticker:*
  light blue 16402

Instructions

1. Cut, score and fold a light blue
   double card (13 x 13 cm).

2. Stick the scrapbook sticker of
   the bear in the middle of the card
   and cut out the heart shape.

3. Cut the hands and feet from a second bear
   sticker and use foam tape to stick them on
   the bear.

4. Stick small decorative patterns from the bear
   sticker sheet in the corners and use gold wavy
   lines to join the corners together. Stick a text
   sticker inside the card (in the middle of the heart).

Hello bears

What you need
- Papicolor card: ice blue (42), bright yellow (10) and cornflower blue (05)
- JEJE mother-of-pearl paper: 85030 and 85080
- JEJE sticker sheet: multicoloured bears 10727
- JEJE sticker sheet: alphabet 10810
- JEJE text sticker: blue 16402

Instructions

1. Cut, score and fold an ice blue double card (14.8 x 10.5 cm). Cut three cornflower blue squares (2.5 x 2.5 cm) and two bright yellow squares (2.5 x 2.5 cm).

2. Cut three squares (3 x 3 cm) out of mother-of-pearl paper (85030) and two squares (3 x 3 cm) out of mother-of-pearl paper (85080). Stick the squares of the same colour on top of each other and stick them on the card.

3. Use the letters from the alphabet sticker sheet to make the word "Hurray".

4. Stick a party bear on top of the middle square and stick a bear's head on top of the other squares.

Stick two balloons on the card and stick a text sticker on the left and right-hand sides.

Edges and corners

Fantasy corners

What you need
- *Papicolor card: cerise (33)*
- *JEJE fantasy paper: 85520*
- *JEJE sticker sheet:*
  ornamental corners 20560

Instructions

1. Cut, score and fold a cerise double card (13 x 13 cm).

2. Cut a square (9 x 9 cm) from fantasy paper and a cerise square (8 x 8 cm). Stick one on top of the other and stick them on the card standing on a corner.

3. Stick four of the same sticker patterns in the corners of the card.

4. Stick four of the same sticker patterns on fantasy paper. Cut them out and use foam tape to stick them in the corners of the square. Stick the inlay of one of the patterns in the middle of the square.

Green corners

Instructions

1. Cut, score and fold a night blue double card (14 x 14 cm).

2. Cut a cornflower blue square (13 x 13 cm) and stick it on the card.

3. Stick the corner patterns and the middle piece onto illusion paper and cut them out. Stick the corner patterns 0.5 cm from the corners of the card and the other piece in the middle of the card.

4. Stick the curls from the sticker pattern around the middle piece and stick small patterns between the four corners.

What you need
- Papicolor card:
  night blue (41) and cornflower blue (05)
- JEJE illusion paper: 85700
- JEJE sticker sheet:
  transparent/silver corners 14791

Roses with lace

What you need
- *Papicolor card: blossom (34)*
- *JEJE illusion paper: 85710*
- *JEJE lace border sticker:*
  salmon 14670
- *JEJE cutting sheet: 34024*
- *JEJE text sticker of your choice*

Instructions

1. Cut, score and fold a blossom double card (14.8 x 10.5 cm). Cut a rectangle (14.8 x 10.4 cm) from illusion paper and stick it inside the card.

2. Choose a lace border from the sticker sheet. Stick it on the card and cut out the openings.

3. Cut the rose branch with a border out of the cutting sheet and make it 3D. Stick it on illusion paper and cut it out leaving a 2 mm wide border.

4. Stick everything in the middle of the card and add a text sticker.

Butterfly corners

Instructions

1. Cut, score and fold a salmon pink double card (14 x 14 cm). Cut a square (13 x 13 cm) out of mother-of-pearl paper and a square (12 x 12 cm) out of fantasy paper. Stick the squares on the card.

2. Stick the butterfly corners on salmon pink card. Cut them out and use foam tape to stick them on the card 0.5 cm from the corners of the fantasy paper.

3. Cut a salmon pink square (7 x 7 cm). Use foam tape to stick it standing on a corner in the middle of the card. Stick four inlays from the corner sticker on this square so that the loops overlap each other slightly.

4. Take four butterflies from the holographic sticker sheet and cover the wings with mother-of-pearl paper. Bend the wings and stick the butterflies in the corners of the square.

What you need
- Papicolor card: salmon pink (25)
- JEJE mother-of-pearl paper: 85010
- JEJE fantasy paper: 85520
- JEJE sticker sheet:
  salmon butterfly corners 14780
- JEJE sticker sheet:
  purple holographic butterflies 17516

Sport

Racing cars

What you need
- *Papicolor card:*
  black (01) and fiesta red (12)
- *JEJE mother-of-pearl paper:*
  85110
- *JEJE sticker sheet:*
  cars 14081
- *JEJE text sticker:*
  congratulations 11001

Instructions

1. Cut, score and fold a black double card (10.5 x 21 cm).

2. Cut a mother-of-pearl strip (21 x 6.5 cm) and stick it on the card. Cut a fiesta red strip (21 x 6.2 cm) and use foam tape to stick it on the other strip. Cut the edges to the shape of the card.

3. Stick stickers of racing cars on the red card. Make the flags from the sticker sheet slightly smaller and stick them at the start and finish lines.

4. Stick a bottle in an ice cooler in the middle of the strip. Start by sticking the text stickers in the top left-hand corner and continue to the other side of the card. Cut the word off at the end and begin again in the bottom left-hand corner and continue until the end of the card.

Footballers

What you need

- *Papicolor card: spring green (08) and pieces of bright yellow, dark blue and white*
- *JEJE mother-of-pearl paper: 85070 and 85130*
- *JEJE sticker sheet: footballs 14010*
- *Chalks: light green and yellow*
- *Grey pencil*

Instructions

1. Cut, score and fold a spring green double card (13 x 13 cm).

2. Tear a strip (6 x 13 cm) of mother-of-pearl paper (85130) and a strip (4 x 13 cm) of mother-of-pearl paper (85070) and apply chalk to both strips. Use foam tape to stick the pieces together and then stick them on the card.

3. Stick stickers of footballers on yellow and blue card and the flag on white card and cut them out.

4. Use line stickers to make a goal and use a grey pencil to draw the net. Use foam tape to stick the footballers and the white flag on the card.

Christmas

Father Christmas

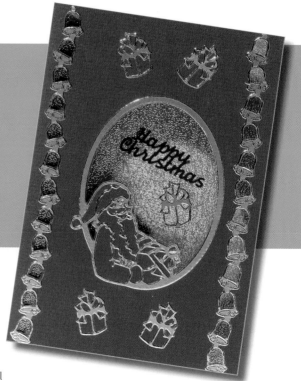

What you need
- *Papicolor card:*
  Christmas green (18)
- *JEJE mother-of-pearl paper: 85100*
- *JEJE sticker sheet:*
  Christmas label 21110
- *JEJE sticker sheet:*
  Christmas bells border 21250
- *JEJE text sticker: green*

Instructions

1. Cut, score and fold a Christmas green double card. Stick a rectangular (10.4 x 14.8 cm) piece of mother-of-pearl paper inside the card.

2. Stick a Christmas bell border on each side of the card. Stick Father Christmas inside an oval frame in the middle of the card and cut out the opening.

3. Stick gift stickers and a text sticker on the card and stick an extra gift inside the card in the middle of the oval.

Christmas trees

Instructions

1. Cut, score and fold a Christmas green double card (10.5 x 14.8 cm).

2. Tear 1 cm off of a strip (6 x 14.8 cm) of mother-of-pearl paper (85000) so that it measures 5 x 14.8 cm and tear 1 cm off of a strip (4.5 x 14.8 cm) mother-of-pearl paper (85130) so that it measures 3.5 x 14 cm. Apply chalks to the tear and use foam tape to stick them on the card.

3. Stick a green and a gold Christmas tree sticker on mother-of-pearl paper (85130) and a silver Christmas tree sticker on circle paper. Cut them out and use foam tape of different thicknesses to stick them on the card with the trunks of the trees between the torn strips of paper.

4. Decorate the card with stars and a text sticker.

Christmas decorations

What you need
- Papicolor card and paper: carnation white (03)
- JEJE circle paper: 85300 and 85320
- JEJE sticker sheet: gold 14020 and red 14026 Christmas decoration
- JEJE text sticker
- Organza ribbon: 1.5 cm

Instructions

1. Cut, score and fold a carnation white double card (10.5 x 21 cm). Cut a corner piece (10.5 x 10.5 cm) from red circle paper and stick it in the bottom right-hand corner of the card.

2. Stick a red and a gold Christmas decoration sticker on the card at different heights. Stick a red Christmas decoration on gold circle paper and a gold Christmas decoration on red circle paper. Cut them out and cut out the middle of the suspension eyes.

3. Take two pieces of Organza ribbon and thread them through the eyes of the Christmas decorations. Stick each ribbon to the card where the eye is and to the inside of the card. Stick a carnation white rectangle (21 x 10.5 cm) over the ribbon inside the card.

4. Cut some pieces of Organza ribbon and use them to hide where the ribbon has been stuck to the card. Add some stars and a text sticker.

30

Mandala

What you need
- *Papicolor card:*
  Christmas red (43) and fiesta red (12)
- *JEJE sticker sheet:*
  gold and gold/green round ornament 21080
- *JEJE text sticker of your choice*
- *Gold thread*

Instructions

1. Cut a piece of Christmas red card (14.8 x 21 cm).
   Score a line 5.2 cm to the left and right of the
   centre and fold the card.

2. Cut three fiesta red rectangles (one of 13.8 x
   9.5 cm and two of 13.8 x 4.3 cm). Stick the large
   rectangle inside the card and stick the two small
   rectangles on the front of the card.

3. Stick the large gold ornament inside the card and
   fill a number of openings with the inlays from the
   large green ornament. Cut a gold ornament in two
   and stick it on the front of the card. Use corner
   stickers to decorate the corners both inside the
   card and on the front of the card.

4. Prick a hole in the left and right-hand sides. Thread
   a gold thread through the holes and close the card
   by tying a bow in the gold thread.

Christmas stars

What you need
- *Papicolor card: night blue (41)*
- *JEJE circle paper: 85310*
- *JEJE sticker sheet: silver/red 21210*
- *JEJE text sticker: red 11029*

Instructions

1. Cut, score and fold a night blue double card (13 x 13 cm). Cut a square (12.5 x 12.5 cm) from circle paper and stick it inside the card.

2. Score the front of the card 7 cm from the fold.

3. Stick star stickers inside the card on the left-hand side, also over the score line, and cut around the stars so that the cut out stars protrude when the front of the card is folded back.

4. Stick red star stickers on the card, also on the circle paper, and stick a text sticker next to the stars.

For JEJE Products please contact your nearest stockist or for more information: Personal Impressions/ Richford LTD Sudbury Suffolk, W. Williams & Son Londen, Habico Leeds, Crafts Too Aldershot Hants, Trimcraft Nottingham and Kars & Co UK.